Friendship

Helen Mortimer & Cristi

BIG WORDS FOR LITTLE PEOPLE

OXFORD
UNIVERSITY PRESS

Fun

When friends get together there is always lots of laughing and giggling.

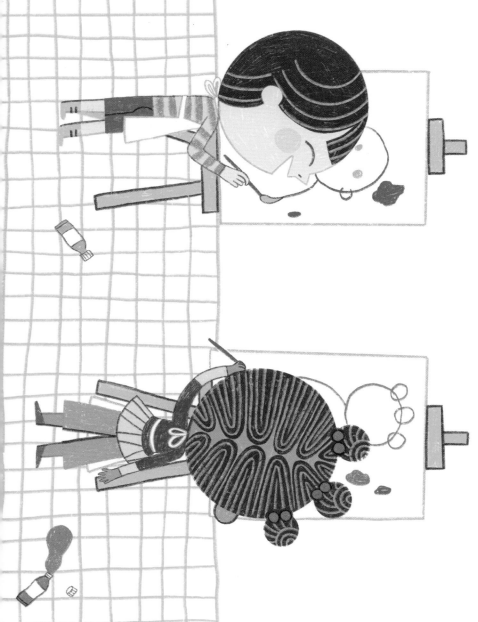

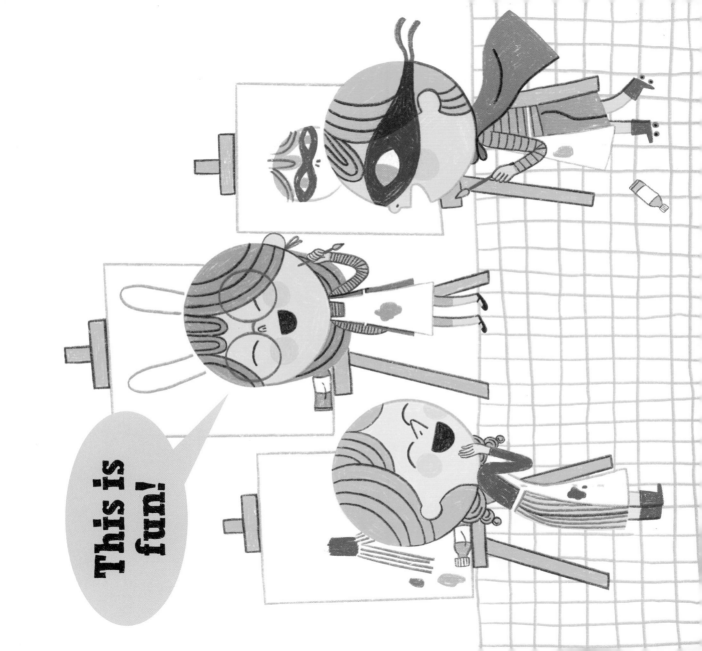

Belonging

When we join in with friends it helps us to feel that we belong.

Respect

We are all unique! Through friendship we can accept each other and respect our differences.

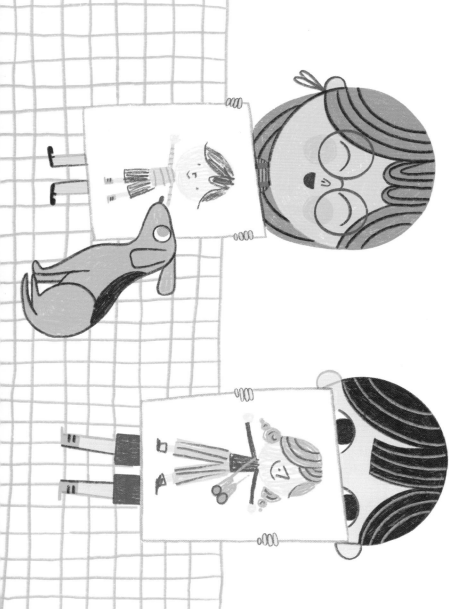

Taking care

You need to look after your friends . . . and you also need to look after your friendships.

That's not very nice

It's okay to fall out but it's important to make up again afterwards.

Share

Share memories, ideas and time with your friends. And don't forget to share treats, too!

Be loyal

True friends know that
they will always stand
by each other.

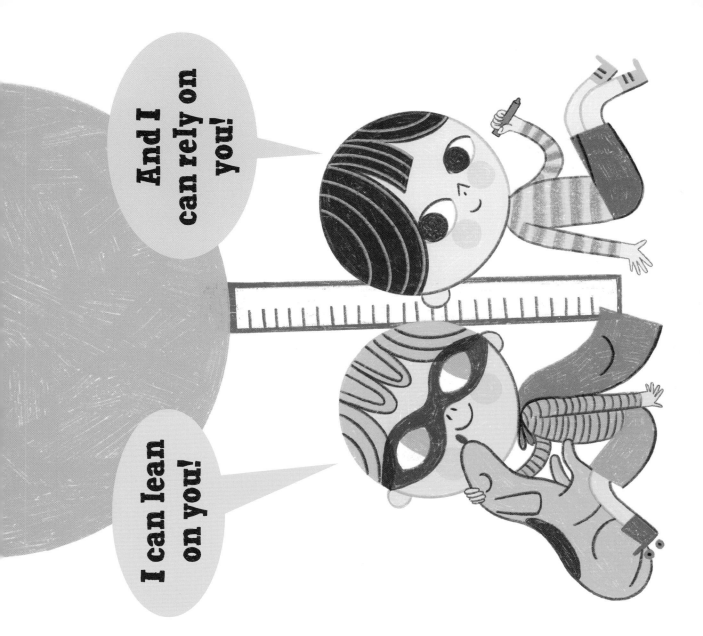

Honesty

If you are open and honest with your friends . . . they will know the real you!

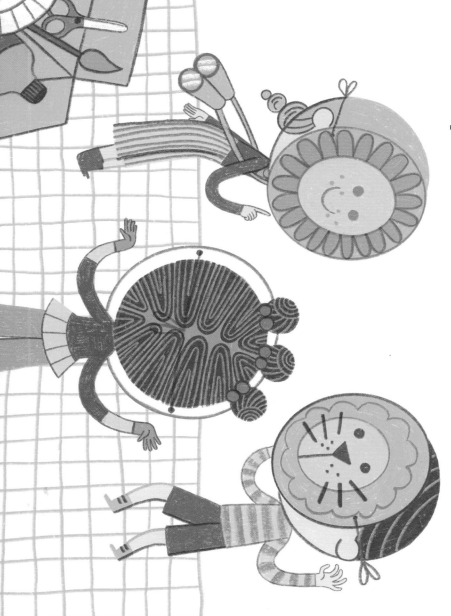

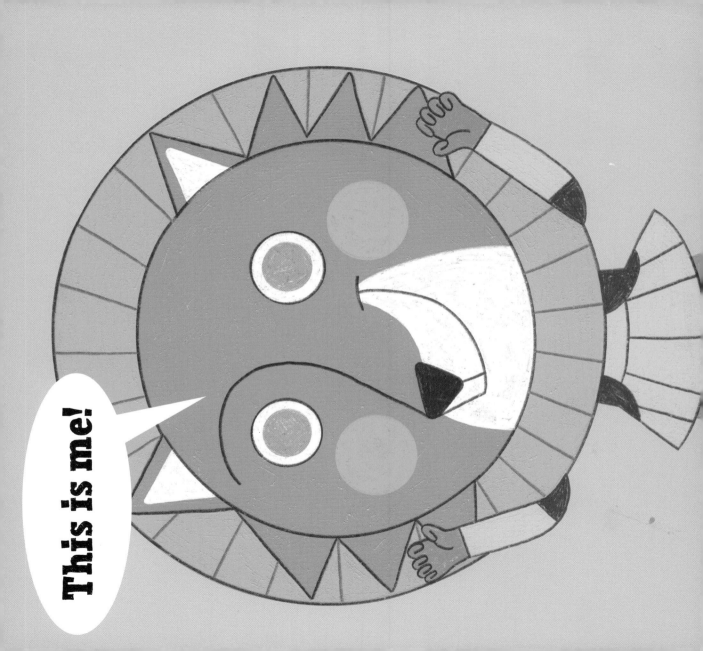

Show

Remember to show your friendship with a wave, a smile or a high-five.

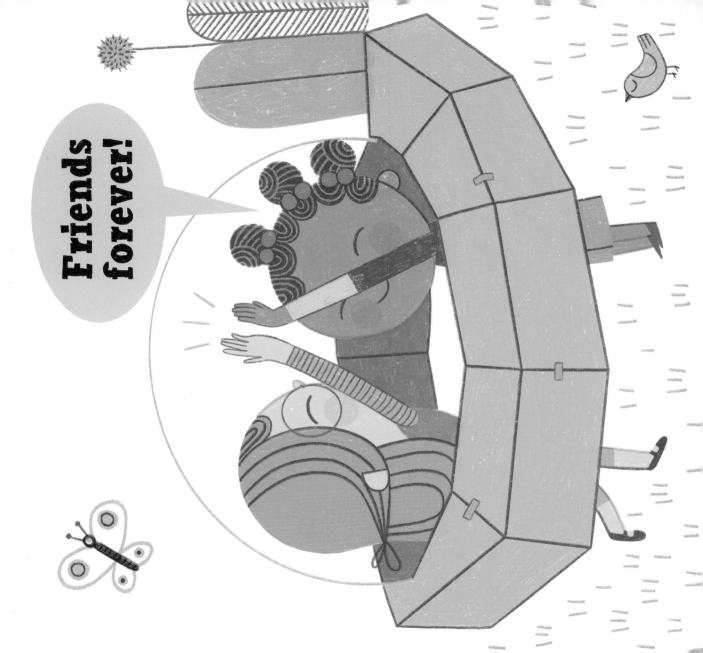

Listen

We trust our friends
and feel safe telling
them everything.

Encourage

Sometimes friends need
help to face new challenges.

A good friend
is always kind.

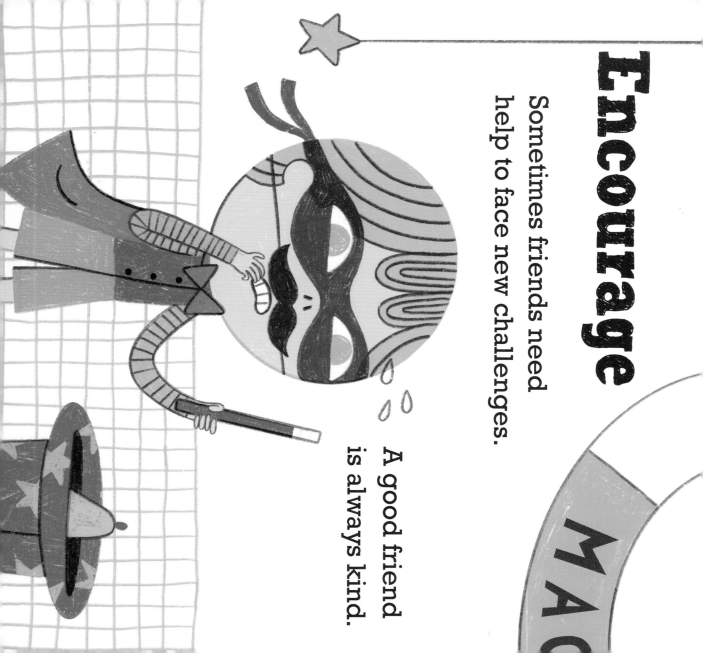

Healthy

Just like healthy food for our bodies, friends are good for us!

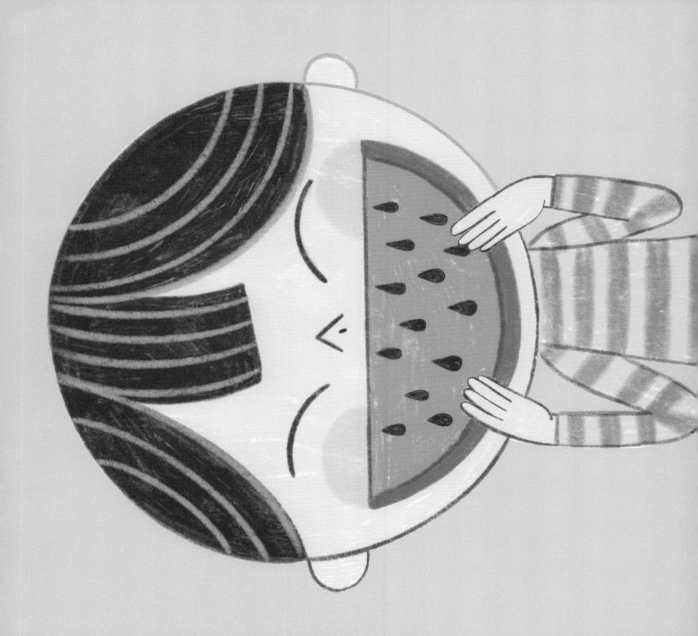

Friendship

Be friendly, make friends and keep friendships.

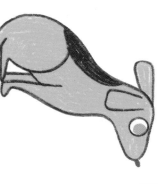

Ten ideas for getting the most from this book

1 Take your time. Sharing a book gives you a precious chance to experience something together and provides so many things to talk about.

2 This book is all about friendship. Talk about your friends and what makes them special.

3 It's also a book about language. Ask each other what words you would use to describe friendship.

4 The illustrations in this book capture various moments in a 'crafternoon'. Why not suggest what might have happened just before each moment and what might happen next?

5 What names would you choose for the children in this book? Do any of them remind you of your own friends?

6 Try to get inside the heads and hearts of each child. Why do they make good friends for each other?

7 This book also considers the challenges when friends fall out and how the strongest friendships always survive these hiccups.

8 By exploring ways to recognize and express how friendships can have a positive impact on everything we do, we hope this book will give children and the adults in their lives the tools they need to make sense of themselves and the world around them.

9 Get crafty! Perhaps this book will inspire you to try some painting, baking, modelling or magic tricks?

10 You could each choose a favourite word about friendship from the book— it will probably be different each time you share the story!

GET CRAFTY!

Glossary

fall out and make up – when you fall out with someone you don't agree with them and when you make up, you become friends again

open – if we are open with someone we are honest and not secretive

respect – if we respect something, we show consideration and we are not rude about it

stand by someone or something – when you stand by a friend, you are on their side

unique – when something is unique, it is the only one of its kind